# Redeemed

## *From the*

# Curse

### Living in the Fullness of God's Blessing

I0080834

# REDEEMED FROM THE CURSE

## LIVING IN THE FULLNESS OF GOD'S BLESSING

### TOM CORNELL

SOZO PUBLISHING

Copyright © 2025 by Tom Cornell

All rights reserved.

No portion of this book may be reproduced in any form or by any means without written permission from the publisher or author, except as permitted by U.S. copyright law. First edition.

Paperback ISBN: 978-1-969882-09-8

Bible quotations are taken from:

The New King James Version® (NKJV). Copyright © 1982 by Thomas Nelson. Used by permission. All rights reserved.

The Holy Bible, New International Version®, NIV®. Copyright © 1973, 1978, 1984, 2011 by Biblica, Inc. Used with permission of Zondervan. All rights reserved worldwide. www.zondervan.com

The ESV® Bible (The Holy Bible, English Standard Version®), © 2001 by Crossway, a publishing ministry of Good News Publishers. Used by permission. All rights reserved."

# CONTENTS

# INTRODUCTION
## THE POWER OF BLESSINGS AND CURSES

All throughout history, people have wrestled with the unseen forces that shape their lives. Some experience an inexplicable favor, an ease in life where doors seem to open effortlessly, while others struggle with continual resistance, frustration, and cycles of destruction. These patterns are not merely coincidental; they are spiritual realities.

Blessings and curses are two opposing forces that determine the course of our lives. They are not myths, nor are they relics of an ancient world. They are spiritual laws that operate in the natural realm, affecting individuals, families, businesses, churches, and even nations. Some experience the fullness of God's blessings because they walk in obedience and alignment with His will, while others unknowingly live under the weight of curses, struggling with repeated misfortune, sickness, and failure.

The good news is that God has provided a way to break free from every curse and step fully into His intended blessing.

Through understanding the reality of blessings and curses, we can shift the trajectory of our lives and the generations that follow.

## The Choice Between Life and Death

God has always given His people a choice: life or death, blessing or curse. In Deuteronomy 30:19, He says:

*"I call heaven and earth to witness against you today, that I have set before you life and death, blessing and curse. Therefore, choose life, that you and your offspring may live." ESV*

This scripture reveals a fundamental truth: blessings and curses are not arbitrary. They do not come by random chance. They are set in motion by spiritual laws, and we have a role in determining which one will define our lives.

Blessings come through obedience to God's word, while curses are the result of disobedience. Many people unknowingly live under a curse—not because they desire to, but because they are unaware of the spiritual principles governing their lives.

This book is designed to bring clarity, break confusion, and empower you to walk fully in the blessings God has prepared for you.

## The Misunderstanding About Generational Curses

One of the most hotly debated topics among believers is the reality of generational curses. Some argue that because of Jesus' finished work on the cross, curses no longer apply to believers. Others misinterpret scriptures, such as Ezekiel 18:20, which states:

*"The soul who sins shall die. The son shall not suffer for the iniquity of the father, nor the father suffer for the iniquity of the son." ESV*

At first glance, this verse may seem to contradict the idea of generational curses. However, context is key. This passage refers to immediate judgment for personal sin, rather than the inherited consequences of iniquity.

If generational curses were not real, why does scripture repeatedly warn about sins passing through bloodlines? Exodus 20:5 states that God visits the iniquity of the fathers upon the children to the third and fourth generation. Lamentations 5:7 says,

*"Our fathers sinned, and are no more; and we bear their iniquities."*
*ESV*

We see this principle play out in the Bible through families bound by cycles of disobedience, poverty, and destruction. Abraham lied about his wife Sarah, and his son Isaac did the same with Rebekah. David fell into sexual sin, and his sons carried the same struggle. These patterns were not random; they were generational in nature.

The cross provided the legal victory over sin, curses, and the power of the enemy. But just as a person must repent and receive salvation for it to be effective, breaking curses also requires intentional action. Jesus has provided freedom, but we must enforce it through faith, repentance, and spiritual warfare.

### Recognizing the Signs of a Curse

Many people struggle through life without realizing they are operating under a curse. Some common signs include:

- Continual financial hardship – No matter how much money is made, it seems to disappear.
- Chronic sickness and disease – A pattern of recurring health issues in a family.
- Repeated relational breakdowns – Divorce, conflict, and rejection that persist across generations.
- Mental torment and emotional distress – Anxiety, depression, or suicidal thoughts running in a family line.
- Barrenness and unfruitfulness – Constant inability to see progress in life, ministry, or business.
- Untimely deaths and tragic accidents – A family history of premature deaths or strange misfortunes.

Curses are not random. They have an entry point. The key to breaking free is understanding how they come and how they can be reversed.

### Jesus Became a Curse to Set Us Free

The power of the gospel is that Jesus took upon Himself every curse so that we might receive the full blessing of God. Galatians 3:13 declares:

*"Christ redeemed us from the curse of the law by becoming a curse for us, for it is written: 'Cursed is everyone who hangs on a tree.'" ESV*

Jesus' sacrifice broke the power of every curse, but many

believers still struggle because they have not applied the finished work of the cross in their lives. Just as salvation must be received through faith and confession, breaking curses also requires action—repentance, renunciation, and aligning with the truth of God's Word.

This book will guide you through the process of recognizing, breaking, and reversing curses over your life. It will also teach you how to step into the fullness of God's blessing and leave a new legacy for future generations.

**A Journey of Transformation**

The truths in this book are not just theoretical—they are practical, biblical, and life-changing. If you are reading this, it is because God is calling you to a higher level of freedom and blessing.

Each chapter will take you deeper into understanding the reality of blessings and curses, how they operate, and most importantly, how to break free.

Are you ready to step into the fullness of God's blessing? Are you prepared to see transformation in your life and family? Then let's begin the journey to freedom.

## 1

# WHAT ARE BLESSINGS AND CURSES?

## THE REALITY OF SPIRITUAL LAWS

From the beginning of time, God established spiritual laws that govern the world. Just as there are physical laws—such as gravity and motion—that determine how the natural world functions, there are spiritual laws that influence our lives. One of the most fundamental laws is the principle of blessings and curses. These are not abstract ideas but real forces that shape individuals, families, and even entire nations.

A blessing is God's divine favor, His supernatural empowerment that causes a person to flourish and succeed according to His purpose. A curse, on the other hand, is the absence of God's favor—resulting in hardship, frustration, and destruction.

These forces do not operate by chance. They are set in motion by actions, words, and spiritual conditions. Deuteronomy 28 lays out a clear contrast between the two:

- Blessings come through obedience to God's commands (Deut. 28:1-14).

- Curses come through disobedience and rebellion (Deut. 28:15-68).

Throughout this book, we will explore how blessings and curses operate, how they affect generations, and how to move from living under a curse into a life of divine blessing.

## Blessings: God's Divine Favor and Empowerment

A blessing is more than a nice word or a well-wishing statement—it is a tangible, spiritual force that brings increase, protection, and divine order. In the Bible, blessings are often spoken by God, priests, parents, and prophets, and they carry the weight of God's authority.

## The Origin of Blessings

Blessings originate from God. The first act of blessing in Scripture is found in Genesis 1:28:

*"And God blessed them, and God said to them, 'Be fruitful and multiply and fill the earth and subdue it, and have dominion over the fish of the sea and over the birds of the heavens and over every living thing that moves on the earth.'" ESV*

God's blessing is linked to fruitfulness, multiplication, and dominion. This means that when a person is blessed, they are empowered to prosper in every area of life. This prosperity is not just financial—it includes spiritual growth, relational harmony, health, and divine protection.

## Types of Blessings in Scripture

*The Blessing of Abraham (Covenantal Blessing)*

- God's covenant with Abraham extended to his descendants (Genesis 12:1-3).
- This blessing includes divine protection, provision, and inheritance.
- Through Christ, believers today are partakers of Abraham's blessing (Galatians 3:14).

*The Priestly Blessing (Spoken Over God's People)*

- In Numbers 6:24-26, God instructs the priests to bless Israel:
- "The Lord bless you and keep you; the Lord make His face shine upon you and be gracious to you; the Lord lift up His countenance upon you and give you peace." NKJV
- This blessing was spoken over the people to invoke divine favor, peace, and security.

*Parental Blessings (Spoken Over Children)*

- Fathers in the Bible regularly blessed their children, releasing destiny over them (Genesis 27:27-29, Genesis 48:13-20).
- A spoken blessing carries generational impact.

*The Blessing of Obedience*

- God promised blessings to those who obey His commands (Deuteronomy 28:1-14).
- These blessings include victory over enemies, fruitfulness, and prosperity in every area.

A life under God's blessing is marked by increase, favor, and supernatural provision. However, just as blessings operate by spiritual laws, so do curses.

## Curses: Spiritual Barriers and Destruction

A curse is the opposite of a blessing. It is a spiritual condition that brings limitation, hardship, and oppression. While many people struggle in life and assume it is normal, some hardships are the result of a curse in operation.

## The Origin of Curses

Curses originate from disobedience, rebellion, and sin. In Genesis 3, after Adam and Eve sinned, God pronounced curses upon them and the earth:

- The ground became cursed – Hardship and toil entered the human experience.
- Pain increased in childbirth – A sign of the curse upon humanity.
- Spiritual death occurred – Separation from God became a reality.

Curses did not originate with God's desire but were a consequence of sin. He desires to bless, but sin brings separation from His blessing and exposes individuals to destruction.

Types of Curses in Scripture

1. Curses from God Due to Disobedience

- Deuteronomy 28:15-68 describes curses for rejecting God's ways.
- These include sickness, poverty, defeat, oppression, and barrenness.

2. Generational Curses (Passed Through Bloodlines)

- Exodus 20:5 states that the iniquity of the fathers can affect descendants to the third and fourth generation.
- Generational patterns of addiction, failure, sickness, and bondage often point to an unbroken curse.

3. Self-Inflicted Curses (Words and Actions)

- Proverbs 18:21 says, "Death and life are in the power of the tongue." NKJV
- Negative words spoken over oneself can invite spiritual oppression.
- Examples include statements like "I'll never succeed" or "Nothing good ever happens to me."

4. Curses from Others (Witchcraft and Evil Declarations)

- In the Bible, Balaam was hired to curse Israel (Numbers 22-24).
- Spoken curses and witchcraft can bring oppression if there is an open door.

5. Cursed Objects and Practices

- Joshua 7 describes how Achan's sin of keeping cursed objects brought destruction to Israel.
- Occult practices, idolatry, and unholy alliances invite curses into a person's life.

**How Blessings and Curses Operate**

Blessings and curses do not happen randomly. They are set in motion through spiritual laws:

- Obedience activates blessings (Deuteronomy 28:1-14).
- Disobedience opens the door to curses (Deuteronomy 28:15-68).
- Generational curses operate through legal rights but can be broken through Christ (Galatians 3:13).
- Curses must be renounced and replaced with blessings (Romans 12:2).

Many people live under a curse because they do not recognize the spiritual laws at work in their lives. But once a curse is broken, the full measure of God's blessing can be released.

**The Good News: Breaking the Curse**

The ultimate solution to breaking every curse is found in Jesus Christ. Galatians 3:13-14 declares:

*"Christ redeemed us from the curse of the law by becoming a curse for us, for it is written: 'Cursed is everyone who hangs on a tree.' So that in Christ Jesus the blessing of Abraham might come to the Gentiles, so that we might receive the promised Spirit through faith." ESV*

Jesus took upon Himself every curse so that we might receive the fullness of God's blessing. However, just as salvation must be received and activated, breaking curses requires repentance, renunciation, and alignment with God's truth.

In the coming chapters, we will dive deeper into how to

recognize, break, and replace curses with blessings. Freedom is available, and God desires His people to walk in full victory.

Are you ready to uncover the areas where the enemy has gained access? Are you ready to break free and walk in the fullness of God's blessing?

Let's move forward into the next chapter and uncover the signs of curses and how they operate in our lives.

## 2

## THE SOURCE OF BLESSINGS

Blessings do not come by accident. They are not merely the result of hard work, intelligence, or good luck. True blessing originates from God Himself. He alone is the source of every good thing, and His Word makes it clear that blessings are released when people align their lives with Him. James 1:17 declares:

> *"Every good and perfect gift is from above, coming down from the Father of lights, who does not change like shifting shadows."* ESV

This means that blessings are not random. They are not dictated by fate or human effort alone. They flow from God's nature and are released when His conditions are met.

The world often promotes a counterfeit version of blessing —one based on wealth, success, and material gain alone. But biblical blessing is far more than financial prosperity. It includes peace, protection, health, purpose, and spiritual authority. It is possible to have worldly riches and still live under a curse, just as it is possible to have little material wealth and yet be truly blessed.

The question is, how do we position ourselves under God's blessing? And how can we ensure that we are receiving His favor rather than walking in opposition to His divine order?

In this chapter, we will explore the different ways God releases blessings and how we can walk in them.

**God's Desire to Bless**

From the beginning, God's heart has been to bless His creation. He is a good Father who delights in the prosperity of His people. Psalm 35:27 says:

*"Let them shout for joy and be glad, who favor my righteous cause; and let them say continually, 'Let the Lord be magnified, who has pleasure in the prosperity of His servant.'" NKJV*

This does not mean that God promises every believer extreme material wealth. Instead, it means that He desires His people to be whole, fruitful, and in alignment with His purpose.

God's blessings are not temporary, nor do they come with sorrow. Proverbs 10:22 states:

*"The blessing of the Lord makes one rich, and He adds no sorrow with it." NKJV*

This is the difference between worldly success and divine blessing. What the world calls "blessing" is often mixed with anxiety, stress, and compromise. But when God blesses, He gives peace along with His provision.

**Covenantal Blessings: The Foundation of Favor**

God's blessings are tied to covenant. A covenant is a divine agreement between God and His people. Throughout Scripture, we see that God releases His blessings through these agreements.

1. The Blessing of Abraham (Genesis 12:1-3, Galatians 3:13-14)

God made a covenant with Abraham, promising him three things:

- Land (inheritance)
- A great nation (generational multiplication)
- A name that would be a blessing to all nations (spiritual influence)

This blessing was not just for Abraham, but for his descendants. Through Christ, all who believe are now partakers of this same blessing (Galatians 3:14). This means that as believers, we are called to inherit the blessings of Abraham—favor, protection, and generational increase.

2. The Blessing of Obedience (Deuteronomy 28:1-14)

God laid out specific blessings for those who obey His commandments:

- Prosperity in all areas of life
- Victory over enemies
- Fruitfulness in family and work

- Divine protection
- Supernatural favor

The key to receiving these blessings is obedience. God does not bless rebellion or partial commitment. He blesses those who walk in His ways.

**3.** The Blessing of the Righteous (Psalm 1:1-3)

Psalm 1 describes the life of a blessed person:

*"Blessed is the man who walks not in the counsel of the wicked, nor stands in the way of sinners, nor sits in the seat of scoffers; but his delight is in the law of the Lord, and on His law he meditates day and night. He is like a tree planted by streams of water that yields its fruit in its season, and its leaf does not wither. In all that he does, he prospers." ESV*

This passage reveals a pattern:

1. What we avoid – The wicked, sinners, and mockers.
2. What we embrace – God's Word and His ways.
3. The result – Stability, fruitfulness, and supernatural prosperity.

**How Blessings Are Released**

**1.** Through the Spoken Word

Blessings are often activated through words. In Scripture, fathers blessed their children through spoken declarations (Genesis 27:27-29). Priests spoke blessings over the people (Numbers 6:24-26). Even Jesus spoke blessings over His disciples (Luke 24:50).

Words carry power. Proverbs 18:21 tells us:

*"Death and life are in the power of the tongue, and those who love it will eat its fruit." ESV*

When we declare God's Word and His promises, we align ourselves with blessing. When we speak negativity, fear, or curses, we can block God's favor in our lives.

## 2. Through Obedience

Obedience to God's commands opens the door to blessing. Jesus said in John 14:15:

*"If you love Me, keep My commandments." NKJV*

Many people pray for blessings but continue to live in ways that contradict God's Word. Blessings are not just given—they are accessed through right living.

## 3. Through Giving

Generosity is a key that unlocks divine blessing. Proverbs 11:25 says:

*"A generous person will prosper; whoever refreshes others will be refreshed." NIV*

Jesus reinforced this in Luke 6:38:

*"Give, and it will be given to you: good measure, pressed down, shaken together, and running over will be put into your bosom." NKJV*

Tithing, offerings, and giving to the poor all invite God's provision into our lives.

**4.** Through Faith

Faith is required to receive God's blessings. Hebrews 11:6 declares:

*"And without faith, it is impossible to please Him, for whoever would draw near to God must believe that He exists and that He rewards those who seek Him." ESV*

Faith is not just belief—it is acting on what God has promised.

**5.** Through Relationship with Jesus

Jesus is the ultimate source of every blessing. Ephesians 1:3 states:

*"Blessed be the God and Father of our Lord Jesus Christ, who has blessed us in Christ with every spiritual blessing in the heavenly places." ESV*

This means that all blessings—spiritual, physical, and material—are found in Him. The more we abide in Christ, the more we position ourselves to receive from Him.

**How to Position Yourself for God's Blessing**

If blessings come from God, how do we position ourselves to receive them? Here are three steps:

**1.** Submit to God's Authority

*James 4:7 says, "Submit yourselves therefore to God. Resist the devil, and he will flee from you." Submission brings protection and favor. ESV*

## 2. Align Your Life with Scripture

*Psalm 119:105 declares: "Your word is a lamp to my feet and a light to my path." Living according to God's Word keeps us on the path of blessing. ESV*

## 3. Walk in Holiness and Faithfulness

*Hebrews 12:14 tells us: "Strive for peace with everyone, and for the holiness without which no one will see the Lord." Holiness attracts the presence and blessing of God. ESV*

## Choose Blessing

Blessings are not random. They are the result of walking with God, obeying His Word, and aligning our lives with His truth. The choice is ours. Deuteronomy 30:19 calls us to action:

*"I have set before you life and death, blessing and curse. Therefore choose life, that you and your offspring may live." ESV*

# 3

---

# THE SOURCE OF CURSES AND THE
# REALITY OF GENERATIONAL CURSES

Just as blessings are a tangible, spiritual force that brings increase and favor, curses are a spiritual force that brings limitation, oppression, and destruction. While many believers recognize the reality of blessings, fewer understand how curses operate, and even fewer know how to break free from them.

A curse is a divine or demonic restriction that hinders the fulfillment of God's promises in a person's life. It can manifest as cycles of failure, chronic illness, financial hardship, broken relationships, and unexplainable misfortune. Unlike mere bad luck, curses have spiritual roots that must be identified and broken for a person to walk in freedom.

Deuteronomy 28 presents a clear contrast between blessings and curses:

- Blessings come through obedience to God's commands (Deut. 28:1-14).

- Curses come through disobedience and rebellion against His ways (Deut. 28:15-68).

Curses are not random or coincidental. They have a source, an entry point, and a legal right. Understanding how they operate is the first step to breaking free.

**The Source of Curses**

1. The Curse of Disobedience (Deuteronomy 28:15-68)

God explicitly warns that rebellion and disobedience bring curses. When people reject God's authority and embrace sin, they open the door for oppression.

Some of the curses listed in Deuteronomy 28 include:

- Sickness and disease (v. 21-22, 27-28, 35).
- Poverty and lack (v. 17-18, 38-40).
- Defeat and oppression (v. 25, 33, 43-44).
- Family breakdown and distress (v. 30-32, 41).

These consequences were not merely for Israel but serve as a warning for all who turn away from God's ways.

2. Generational Curses (Exodus 20:5, Numbers 14:18)

One of the most misunderstood spiritual principles is that sin does not only affect the one who commits it—it can impact generations.

Exodus 20:5 states:

*"You shall not bow down to them or serve them, for I, the Lord your*

*God, am a jealous God, visiting the iniquity of the fathers on the children to the third and fourth generation of those who hate Me." NKJV*

This means that the sinful choices of one generation can create spiritual and natural consequences for future generations. We see this reality in families where cycles of:

- Addiction
- Divorce
- Poverty
- Chronic illness
- Mental torment
- Premature death

...continue from one generation to the next.

Addressing the Misuse of Ezekiel 18:20

Some argue that generational curses no longer apply today, citing Ezekiel 18:20:

*"The soul who sins shall die. The son shall not suffer for the iniquity of the father, nor the father suffer for the iniquity of the son." ESV*

However, this verse refers to personal judgment, not generational consequences. In the Old Testament, there were times when God executed immediate judgment on families for one person's sin (e.g., Achan's family in Joshua 7). But Ezekiel 18 clarifies that God will no longer bring immediate judgment on children for their parents' sins.

This does not mean that generational curses no longer exist —it simply means God is not executing judgment in the same way. However, spiritual consequences still pass through blood-lines unless they are broken through repentance and the power of Christ.

**3. Self-Inflicted Curses (Proverbs 18:21, Matthew 12:36-37)**

Words carry power. Many people unknowingly curse themselves through their speech.

Proverbs 18:21 says:

*"Death and life are in the power of the tongue, and those who love it will eat its fruit." ESV*

Examples of self-inflicted curses include:

- "Nothing good ever happens to me."
- "I'll never get out of debt."
- "I always get sick this time of year."
- "I'm just like my father—always a failure."

Jesus warned that we will give an account for every idle word spoken (Matthew 12:36-37). If we align our words with negativity, fear, or failure, we empower those realities in our lives.

**4. Curses From Others (Witchcraft, Occult Practices, and Evil Declarations)**

The Bible warns against curses spoken by others, especially through witchcraft, divination, and demonic influence.

- Balaam was hired to curse Israel (Numbers 22-24).
- Goliath cursed David by his gods (1 Samuel 17:43).

- Jezebel operated through witchcraft to destroy God's prophets (1 Kings 19:2).

Today, many people suffer under word curses spoken by parents, teachers, authority figures, or enemies. These can include:

- "You'll never amount to anything."
- "You were a mistake."
- "You're going to end up just like your father/mother."

Such statements, when accepted, can become strongholds that influence a person's life.

## 5. Cursed Objects and Unholy Alliances

The Bible warns against bringing cursed objects into one's home.

Deuteronomy 7:26 says:

*"You shall not bring an abominable thing into your house and become devoted to destruction like it. You shall utterly detest and abhor it, for it is devoted to destruction." ESV*

Objects tied to idolatry, witchcraft, and occult practices can invite demonic influence. This includes:

- Occult books, tarot cards, Ouija boards.
- Statues or items dedicated to false gods.
- Jewelry or symbols linked to witchcraft.

Similarly, forming ungodly partnerships can lead to curses.

Malachi 2:11 warns that intermarrying with idol worshipers led to judgment upon Israel.

## How Curses Operate

### 1. Curses Create Legal Rights for Demonic Oppression

Demons operate under legal rights. If a curse is in place, the enemy has access to afflict and hinder a person's life.

### 2. Curses Cause Repetitive Cycles

Many people find themselves repeating the same patterns of failure, addiction, or broken relationships. These are often the result of an unbroken curse.

### 3. Curses Remain Until They Are Broken

Curses do not simply disappear with time. They must be confronted, renounced, and broken through the power of Jesus Christ.

## The Good News: Curses Can Be Broken

Many believers struggle under the weight of curses because they do not realize that Jesus has already provided a way of escape. Galatians 3:13-14 declares:

*"Christ redeemed us from the curse of the law by becoming a curse for us, for it is written: 'Cursed is everyone who is hanged on a tree.'" ESV*

Jesus took upon Himself every curse so that we might

receive God's blessing. However, just as salvation must be received, the breaking of curses requires:

1. Recognizing the curse – Identifying patterns in one's life.
2. Repenting for any sin that opened the door – Closing demonic access points.
3. Renouncing the curse in Jesus' name – Breaking agreement with darkness.
4. Replacing the curse with God's truth – Walking in obedience and blessing.

**4**

## SIGNS YOU ARE UNDER A CURSE

Many people go through life facing repeated struggles, setbacks, and oppression without understanding that they may be under a curse. They assume that their problems are normal, a result of bad luck, or simply life's hardships. However, Scripture makes it clear that when a curse is in operation, it creates patterns of destruction that are not random but spiritual in nature. Hosea 4:6 says:

*"My people are destroyed for lack of knowledge." NKJV*

One of the enemy's greatest strategies is to keep believers ignorant of spiritual realities. If people do not recognize that a curse is affecting their lives, they will continue to suffer under it without ever seeking deliverance. This chapter will help you identify whether a curse is at work and how to discern patterns that indicate spiritual bondage.

**How to Identify a Curse**

A curse is not just a single instance of hardship. Rather, it is a recurring cycle of misfortune, affliction, or destruction that seems resistant to change. It often follows family bloodlines or appears as a persistent struggle in a person's life, despite their best efforts to overcome it.

Deuteronomy 28:15-68 outlines the consequences of curses, and many of the signs listed there still manifest in people's lives today. If you recognize one or more of these signs in your own life, it is possible that a curse is in operation.

1. Chronic Financial Struggles and Poverty

- No matter how much money is earned, it always seems to disappear.
- Constant job losses, unexpected expenses, and failed business ventures.
- Inability to get ahead financially despite hard work and wise planning.
- Family history of financial instability, debt, and lack.

Deuteronomy 28:17 warns that a curse can cause a person's work and finances to be unfruitful:

*"Cursed shall be your basket and your kneading bowl." NKJV*

2. Constant Health Problems and Sickness

- Recurring illnesses that doctors cannot fully diagnose or cure.
- Chronic pain, migraines, autoimmune diseases, and mysterious ailments.
- Family history of the same sickness affecting multiple generations.
- Frequent miscarriages or infertility.

Deuteronomy 28:22 states:

*"The Lord will strike you with wasting disease, with fever and inflammation, with scorching heat and drought, and with blight and mildew, which will pursue you until you perish." Paraphrase NIV/ESV*

## 3. Repeated Accidents and Unnatural Deaths

- A pattern of car accidents, freak injuries, or near-death experiences.
- Multiple family members dying young, especially in tragic circumstances.
- Suicides or premature deaths that seem to be a generational pattern.

Deuteronomy 28:29 describes a curse where people stumble through life without direction:

*"You shall grope at noonday, as the blind grope in darkness, and you shall not prosper in your ways. And you shall be only oppressed and robbed continually, and there shall be no one to help you." ESV*

## 4. Broken Marriages and Family Dysfunction

- A history of divorce, adultery, or unhealthy relationships across generations.
- Ongoing conflicts between parents and children, or sibling rivalry.
- Domestic violence, abandonment, or family separations.
- An inability to maintain stable and loving relationships.

Malachi 2:14 warns that breaking marriage covenants can bring a curse upon a person's life:

*"The Lord was witness between you and the wife of your youth, to whom you have been faithless, though she is your companion and your wife by covenant." ESV*

5. Repeated Failures and Blocked Opportunities

- Every attempt at success seems to be blocked or met with frustration.
- Promotions and breakthroughs are constantly delayed or denied.
- A cycle of working hard but never seeing lasting fruit.
- Generational struggles in education, career, or ministry.

Deuteronomy 28:23-24 describes how curses can cause failure in every area of life:

*"The heavens over your head shall be bronze, and the earth under you shall be iron. The Lord will make the rain of your land powder. From heaven dust shall come down on you until you are destroyed."*
*ESV*

6. Mental Torment and Emotional Bondage

- Depression, anxiety, and extreme mood swings.
- Persistent fear, paranoia, or suicidal thoughts.
- Hearing voices, seeing dark shadows, or experiencing night terrors.
- Generational history of mental illness.

Deuteronomy 28:28 warns:

*"The Lord will strike you with madness and blindness and confusion of mind." ESV*

7. Addictions and Self-Destructive Behavior

- Substance abuse (drugs, alcohol, smoking) that runs in the family.
- Addictions to pornography, gambling, or destructive habits.
- An inability to break free from certain sins despite trying repeatedly.

Isaiah 5:11 warns of curses related to drunkenness and addiction:

*"Woe to those who rise early in the morning, that they may run after strong drink, who tarry late into the evening as wine inflames them!" ESV*

8. Oppression and Unnatural Resistance to Spiritual Growth

- An inability to pray, read the Bible, or grow spiritually.
- Feeling disconnected from God despite a desire to serve Him.
- Constant backsliding or spiritual dryness.
- Repeated attacks of discouragement, heaviness, or confusion.

Isaiah 61:3 describes how God delivers people from a "spirit of heaviness"—a form of spiritual oppression that keeps people bound.

**Recognizing the Difference Between Natural Struggles and a Curse**

Not every hardship in life is a curse. Some struggles are part of spiritual growth, discipline, or simply life's challenges. However, there are key signs that differentiate ordinary difficulties from the operation of a curse:

- Curses are persistent – The problem doesn't go away, even after repeated efforts to fix it.
- Curses are generational – The same issue appears in parents, grandparents, and children.
- Curses resist prayer – Even after seeking God, the struggle remains or intensifies.
- Curses feel unnatural – They defy logic, reason, and normal circumstances.

If these patterns are evident in your life, it is time to take action and break free.

**Breaking the Cycle of Curses**

The good news is that curses are not permanent—they can be broken! Jesus has already provided the victory, but it requires faith, repentance, and spiritual warfare to enforce that victory.

Now that you understand the signs of a curse, take a moment to reflect:

1. Do any of these patterns describe your life or your family's history?
2. Have you experienced unexplained resistance, repeated failure, or oppression?

3. Have you tried everything in your own strength but found no lasting breakthrough?
4. If you answered yes to any of these, it is time to break the cycle and walk in freedom

# 5

## HOW CURSES ENTER

Curses do not randomly affect people; they have specific entry points that give them legal access to operate in a person's life or bloodline. Just as blessings are activated through obedience to God, curses are set in motion through sin, disobedience, and spiritual agreements with darkness.

The enemy cannot place a curse on someone without a legal right. Proverbs 26:2 confirms this:

*"Like a sparrow in its flitting, like a swallow in its flying, a curse that is causeless does not alight." ESV*

This means that curses require an entry point to take effect. These open doors can come through personal sin, generational iniquity, negative words, or demonic covenants. In this chapter, we will explore the four primary ways curses enter and how to close these doors.

### 1. Personal Sin and Disobedience – Opening Doors to Oppression

The most direct way a curse can enter a person's life is through willful disobedience to God's commands. Deuteronomy 28:15-68 outlines a long list of curses that result from turning away from God's ways.

Key Verses on Sin and Curses:

*Deuteronomy 28:15 – "But if you will not obey the voice of the Lord your God or be careful to do all His commandments and His statutes that I command you today, then all these curses shall come upon you and overtake you." ESV*

*Isaiah 59:2 – "But your iniquities have made a separation between you and your God, and your sins have hidden His face from you so that He does not hear." ESV*

Common Sins That Open the Door to Curses:

1. Idolatry and False Worship – Involvement in the occult, worship of false gods, or reliance on horoscopes, psychics, or spiritualism.
2. Rebellion Against God's Word – Deliberate disobedience, pride, and rejecting biblical truth.
3. Sexual Sin – Adultery, fornication, pornography, incest, and perversion.
4. Unforgiveness and Bitterness – Holding grudges and refusing to forgive gives the enemy legal ground (Matthew 6:14-15).
5. Lying and Deception – A lifestyle of dishonesty, fraud, or manipulation invites spiritual consequences (Proverbs 6:16-19).
6. Stealing and Dishonoring Authority – This includes financial dishonesty, dishonoring parents, and rejecting godly leadership.

7. Covenant Breaking – Divorce, broken vows, and violating spiritual commitments can bring relational and generational curses.

Breaking the Curse of Personal Sin:

The good news is that every sin can be repented of and forgiven.

Prayer of Repentance:

*"Father, I repent of every sin that has given the enemy access to my life. I renounce disobedience, rebellion, and every act that dishonored You. I ask for Your forgiveness and the cleansing power of the blood of Jesus. I break the legal right of every curse associated with my past sins, and I declare that I am free in Christ. Amen."*

## 2. Words Spoken Over Your Life – Curses from Authority Figures or Self-Inflicted Vows

The Bible teaches that words have power—they can either bless or curse. Many people unknowingly live under a word curse spoken by parents, teachers, spiritual leaders, or even their own mouths.

Key Verses on the Power of Words:

*Proverbs 18:21 – "Death and life are in the power of the tongue, and those who love it will eat its fruits." ESV*

*James 3:8-10 – "But no human being can tame the tongue. It is a restless evil, full of deadly poison... From the same mouth come blessing and cursing. My brothers, these things ought not to be so." ESV*

Types of Word Curses:

1. Curses Spoken by Parents or Authority Figures – Words like "You'll never amount to anything" or "You're a failure" can shape a person's life.
2. Self-Imposed Curses – Speaking defeat over yourself (e.g., "I'll never be happy," "I always get sick," "Nothing good ever happens to me").
3. Curses from Others (Witchcraft or Negative Declarations) – People can pronounce curses intentionally through spells, hexes, or evil declarations.
4. Curses from Inner Vows – Making negative declarations like "I'll never trust anyone again" or "I will never love again" can create spiritual barriers.

Breaking Word Curses:

Every curse spoken over you must be renounced and replaced with God's truth.

Prayer to Break Word Curses:

*"In the name of Jesus, I break every negative word spoken over my life. I cancel every lie, every curse, and every word of defeat. I declare that I am blessed, favored, and chosen by God. I reject every false identity placed upon me, and I embrace my true identity in Christ. Amen."*

## 3. Generational Curses – How Iniquity Passes Down Unless Broken

Many people experience repeated struggles that can be traced through multiple generations. This is because sin and iniquity create spiritual patterns that pass from parents to children.

Key Verses on Generational Curses:

*Exodus 20:5 – "For I, the Lord your God, am a jealous God, visiting the iniquity of the fathers on the children to the third and the fourth generation of those who hate Me." NKJV*

*Lamentations 5:7 – "Our fathers sinned, and are no more; and we bear their iniquities." NKJV*

Common Generational Curses:

- Poverty and Financial Struggles
- Chronic Illnesses and Premature Death
- Addiction (Alcoholism, Drugs, Gambling, etc.)
- Mental Health Disorders and Suicide
- Sexual Immorality and Divorce
- Witchcraft and Occult Practices in Family History
- Breaking Generational Curses:

Generational curses remain in place until someone stands in the gap and renounces them.

Prayer to Break Generational Curses:

*"Father, I repent for the sins of my ancestors. I break every generational curse in my bloodline and cancel the enemy's legal right over my family. I renounce the iniquities of my forefathers, and I declare that I am no longer bound by their sins. The blood of Jesus sets me free, and I establish a new generational blessing over my family. Amen."*

## 4. Demonic Covenants and Witchcraft – The Impact of Occult Involvement in Family Bloodlines

Many people suffer under curses because their ancestors or they themselves have entered into demonic agreements. This includes direct or indirect involvement with the occult, witch-craft, or false religions.

Key Verses on Occult Involvement and Curses:

*Deuteronomy 18:10-12 – "There shall not be found among you anyone who burns his son or his daughter as an offering, anyone who practices divination or tells fortunes or interprets omens, or a sorcerer." ESV*

*Leviticus 19:31 – "Do not turn to mediums or necromancers; do not seek them out, and so make yourselves unclean by them." ESV*

Breaking Demonic Covenants:

If you or your ancestors have engaged in witchcraft, Freemasonry, false religions, or occult practices, you must renounce these ties.

Prayer to Renounce Demonic Covenants:

*"In Jesus' name, I renounce every demonic covenant made by me or my ancestors. I break every agreement with witchcraft, false religion, and occult practices. I cancel every demonic assignment against my life and declare that I belong to Jesus Christ. Amen."*

### Close Every Door and Walk in Freedom

Curses enter through legal access points, but they can be

broken through repentance, renunciation, and the blood of Jesus. In the next chapter, we will discuss the power of Christ to break every curse and establish lasting freedom!

Get ready—your breakthrough is near!

# 6

# THE POWER OF CHRIST TO BREAK CURSES

The good news of the Gospel is that no curse is permanent —Jesus has already provided the way for deliverance. While curses may enter through sin, generational iniquity, spoken words, or demonic covenants, the power of Christ nullifies every legal claim the enemy has. Galatians 3:13-14 declares:

*"Christ redeemed us from the curse of the law by becoming a curse for us, for it is written: 'Cursed is everyone who hangs on a tree,' so that in Christ Jesus the blessing of Abraham might come to the Gentiles, so that we might receive the promised Spirit through faith." ESV*

This passage reveals three powerful truths:

1. Jesus took the curse upon Himself – He became a substitute, carrying every curse we deserved.
2. He legally broke the curse of sin and death – The enemy no longer has authority over those in Christ.
3. He transferred us into blessing – We are no longer

bound to generational iniquity but can receive the
blessings of Abraham.

Many believers know they are saved, but they do not walk
in their full spiritual inheritance because they have not applied
Christ's finished work to every area of their lives. This chapter
will explain how the blood of Jesus legally cancels curses and
how to enforce your freedom through faith, repentance, and
confession.

## I. Galatians 3:13 – Jesus Became a Curse for Us

In the Old Testament, breaking God's law resulted in curses,
including sickness, poverty, and oppression (Deuteronomy
28:15-68). The law exposed sin but could not fully remove its
effects—only Jesus could do that.

How Did Jesus Break the Power of Curses?

1. He took the curse upon Himself – Every curse that
   should have fallen on us was placed on Jesus at the
   cross.
2. He became the final sacrifice – No more blood
   sacrifices are needed; His sacrifice was once and for
   all (Hebrews 9:26).
3. He reversed the consequences of the fall – Adam's
   sin brought death and destruction, but Jesus
   brought life and restoration (Romans 5:17).

Because Jesus became the curse, every person in Him is no
longer legally bound by the power of generational, spoken, or
self-inflicted curses. However, deliverance is enforced by faith
—we must apply what Jesus has done to experience freedom.

## 2. The Blood of Jesus as Our Legal Deliverance

The power of the blood of Jesus is the strongest spiritual weapon against curses. In the Old Testament, the blood of sacrifices temporarily covered sin, but the blood of Jesus permanently removes it. Revelation 12:11 states:

*"And they overcame him by the blood of the Lamb and by the word of their testimony." NKJV*

The blood of Jesus does five things to break curses:

1. Cleanses from Sin (1 John 1:7)

Sin gives curses legal access. The blood of Jesus washes away sin and removes that access point.

2. Cancels the Enemy's Legal Right (Colossians 2:14-15)

The enemy operates through legal accusations, but Jesus erased every claim against us through His blood.

3. Breaks Generational Iniquity (Hebrews 9:14)

The blood of Jesus goes deep into generational bloodlines and washes away inherited sins.

4. Destroys the Works of the Devil (1 John 3:8)

The blood of Jesus renders demonic strongholds powerless, cutting off their ability to operate.

5. Redeems Us from Every Curse (Galatians 3:13-14)

The blood of Jesus transfers us out of the curse and into the blessing of Abraham.

Because of His blood, we no longer belong to the curse—we belong to the Kingdom of God.

### 3. Freedom Through Repentance and Confession

Although Jesus has legally broken every curse, we must enforce our freedom. Just as salvation must be received through confession, breaking curses requires:

1. Identifying areas where curses have operated.
2. Repenting for any sins or agreements that opened the door.
3. Declaring our freedom in Christ.

Step 1: Confessing the Power of Christ's Blood

Declaration:

*"Father, I thank You that the blood of Jesus has set me free. I declare that every curse over my life is broken. The blood of Jesus washes away every legal claim of the enemy. I am redeemed, cleansed, and fully delivered in Jesus' name!"*

Step 2: Repenting for Open Doors

- If personal sin allowed a curse, repent and renounce it.
- If a generational curse was inherited, stand in the gap and break it.

Prayer of Repentance:

*"Father, I repent for any sin in my life or my family that opened the door to curses. I renounce every generational iniquity, spoken curse, and personal rebellion. I ask for Your forgiveness and cleansing through the blood of Jesus. I turn fully to You and reject every form of darkness. In Jesus' name, Amen."*

Step 3: Declaring Deliverance Over Your Life

Declaration:

*"I decree and declare that I am free from every curse. I am covered by the blood of Jesus, and no demonic force has power over me. I reject every lie of the enemy, and I walk in the fullness of God's blessing. In Jesus' name, Amen!"*

**Breaking Specific Types of Curses**

**1. Breaking Generational Curses**

*"In the name of Jesus, I break every generational curse in my family line. I renounce the sins of my ancestors and cancel every demonic assignment against my bloodline. The blood of Jesus washes my lineage clean, and I establish a new legacy of blessing. My family and descendants will serve the Lord, in Jesus' name!"*

**2. Breaking Word Curses**

*"I cancel every negative word spoken over my life. I break the power of every lie, curse, and false identity placed on me. I declare that I am who God says I am—blessed, chosen, and favored. No weapon formed against me shall prosper!"*

**3. Breaking Curses from Witchcraft and the Occult**

*"I renounce every demonic covenant made knowingly or unknowingly. I break every curse connected to witchcraft, divination, or false religion. I cut off every soul tie to darkness and declare that Jesus Christ is my only Lord. Every demonic assignment is destroyed in Jesus' name!"*

## Live in the Blessing of Christ

Breaking curses is not just about freedom from oppression —it is about stepping into divine blessing. Jesus did not just remove the curse; He restored the blessings of Abraham to those who believe (Galatians 3:14).

## Next Steps to Walk in Freedom:

1. Stay rooted in God's Word – The truth keeps you free (John 8:32).
2. Live a lifestyle of prayer and obedience – Daily communion with God keeps doors closed.
3. Declare your new identity – Continually speak and believe the blessings of the Lord.

## Final Declaration:

*"I declare that every curse over my life is broken! I am no longer bound by the past—I walk in the full blessing of Jesus Christ. My family, my finances, and my future are covered by His blood. I will not return to bondage, but I will live in victory, favor, and divine purpose! In Jesus' name, Amen!"*

# 7

# STEPS TO BREAKING CURSES

O nce a curse has been identified, it must be intentionally broken. Jesus has already provided the way for deliverance, but we must enforce our freedom by applying biblical principles. Just as salvation is received through faith and confession, breaking curses requires repentance, renunciation, and spiritual warfare.

This chapter will provide a step-by-step guide to breaking curses and walking in complete victory.

**Step 1:** Identify the Curse – Ask the Holy Spirit for Revelation

Many people struggle under curses without realizing it. The enemy thrives in ignorance and deception, keeping people bound by hiding the root cause of their struggles.

How to Identify a Curse:

1. Look for Repeated Patterns – Is there a cycle of

sickness, failure, financial struggle, addiction, or broken relationships in your family?

2. Examine Your Life Through Scripture – Deuteronomy 28 outlines both blessings (verses 1-14) and curses (verses 15-68). Compare your experiences to God's Word.
3. Pray for Revelation – Ask the Holy Spirit to reveal hidden sources of curses.

Prayer for Revelation:

*"Holy Spirit, I ask for Your guidance. Show me any area of my life that is under a curse. Reveal hidden agreements, generational iniquities, or spoken words that have given the enemy access. Let Your light expose every darkness. In Jesus' name, Amen."*

**Step 2:** Repent and Renounce Open Doors – Confess Sins and Cancel Legal Rights

Curses operate through legal access. If sin, rebellion, or demonic agreements exist, they must be repented of and renounced.

What to Repent From:

1. Personal Sin – Any disobedience, bitterness, unforgiveness, or rebellion that has opened the door.
2. Generational Sin – The iniquities of your ancestors that may have brought curses.
3. Demonic Agreements – Any past involvement in witchcraft, false religions, or secret covenants.

Prayer of Repentance:

"Father, I come before You in the name of Jesus. I repent for every sin that has given the enemy access to my life. I renounce rebellion, idolatry, and every act of disobedience. I also stand in the gap for my family and repent for the sins of my ancestors. I break agreement with every generational iniquity and ask for the cleansing power of the blood of Jesus to wash over my life. In Jesus' name, Amen."

**Step 3:** Forgive Others – Unforgiveness Keeps Curses in Place

Many curses remain because of unforgiveness. Jesus warned that if we do not forgive others, we will not be forgiven (Matthew 6:14-15). Holding onto offense gives the enemy a legal right to afflict us.

Signs of Unforgiveness:

- Holding grudges and replaying past hurts.
- Struggling with bitterness or resentment.
- Avoiding people who have wronged you.

Prayer of Forgiveness:

*"Lord, I choose to forgive those who have wronged me. I release every offense and reject bitterness. I bless those who have hurt me, and I ask for Your healing in my heart. As I forgive others, I receive Your forgiveness and freedom. In Jesus' name, Amen."*

**Step 4:** Declare Your Deliverance in Christ – Break Agreements with Darkness

Once repentance has taken place, you must verbally renounce the curse and declare your freedom.

How to Break Agreements with Darkness:

1. Verbally reject every curse.
2. Declare that the blood of Jesus has set you free.
3. Command demonic spirits to leave.

Prayer of Renunciation and Deliverance:

*"In the name of Jesus, I renounce every curse that has been spoken over my life. I break the power of every generational curse, word curse, and demonic assignment. I reject every lie of the enemy and declare that I am free by the blood of Jesus. I cancel every legal right the enemy has claimed over me, and I command every spirit of oppression, affliction, and bondage to leave now! I belong to Jesus Christ, and no curse has power over me! Amen."*

Biblical Declarations for Deliverance:

- "No weapon formed against me shall prosper" (Isaiah 54:17).
- "Christ redeemed us from the curse of the law" (Galatians 3:13).
- "The Son has set me free, and I am free indeed" (John 8:36).

**Step 5:** Replace the Curse with God's Blessing – Walk in Obedience and Faith

Freedom is not just about breaking curses—it's about stepping into blessing. When a curse is removed, it must be replaced with God's truth.

How to Walk in Blessing:

1. Speak God's promises daily – Declare Deuteronomy 28:1-14 over your life.
2. Align Your Life with God's Word – Obey His commands and live righteously.
3. Reject Negative Words and Thoughts – Do not allow fear or doubt to re-enter.

Prayer to Establish Blessing:

*"Father, I thank You for my deliverance. I receive the fullness of Your blessing over my life. I declare that I am blessed, favored, and protected. I walk in divine health, financial provision, and supernatural peace. No curse will ever touch me again. My family is covered under the blood of Jesus, and I will leave a legacy of faith and righteousness. In Jesus' name, Amen!"*

Daily Declarations of Blessing:

1. "I am the head and not the tail" (Deuteronomy 28:13).
2. "I will lend and not borrow" (Deuteronomy 28:12).
3. "The Lord is my protector and my shield" (Psalm 91:4-5).

**Enforce Your Freedom Daily**

Breaking curses is not just a one-time event—it is a lifestyle of freedom. The enemy will attempt to test your faith, but you must stand firm in your deliverance.

**Final Steps to Ensure Freedom:**

1. Daily Prayer and Scripture Reading – Keep renewing your mind.

2. Reject Fear and Doubt – Do not allow the enemy to regain access.
3. Stay in a Community of Faith – Surround yourself with believers who walk in victory.

## Final Declaration of Freedom

*"I declare that I am free in Jesus' name! Every curse is broken, and I walk in the fullness of God's blessing. No demonic force has power over me. I will not return to bondage, but I will live in victory, peace, and divine purpose. I am a child of God, and my future is blessed! Amen!"*

# 8

## DELIVERANCE FROM GENERATIONAL CURSES
### BREAKING THE CYCLE IN YOUR BLOODLINE

Many believers struggle with patterns of bondage that do not originate from their own choices but from generational curses—spiritual consequences passed down through family lines. These inherited struggles can manifest in repeated cycles of poverty, sickness, addiction, divorce, or premature death.

The good news is that one person's breakthrough can shift an entire family. When a believer recognizes a generational curse and takes spiritual authority, they can break the cycle and establish a new legacy of blessing.

*"For I, the LORD your God, am a jealous God, visiting the iniquity of the fathers upon the children to the third and fourth generations of those who hate Me, but showing mercy to thousands, to those who love Me and keep My commandments." Exodus 20:5-6 NKJV*

This passage reveals that sin can pass down through generations—but so can blessing! The choice is ours.

This chapter will equip you with prayers, declarations, and steps to break generational curses and replace them with God's blessing for future generations.

**Step 1:** Identify the Generational Curse

A generational curse is recognized by patterns of oppression that repeat through family lines.

Common Signs of Generational Curses:

- Poverty and Financial Struggles – A history of debt, lack, or financial failure.
- Chronic Illnesses – Family patterns of cancer, heart disease, mental illness, or genetic disorders.
- Addiction – Alcoholism, drug abuse, gambling, or destructive behaviors.
- Sexual Immorality and Broken Relationships – Divorce, adultery, abuse, or perversion.
- Premature Death and Tragedy – Unnatural accidents, suicides, or sudden illnesses in family lines.
- Mental Health Issues – Depression, fear, schizophrenia, or generational cycles of torment.
- Involvement in the Occult – Witchcraft, Freemasonry, false religions, or secret societies.

If any of these patterns are evident in your parents, grandparents, or great-grandparents, it is likely that a generational curse is in operation.

**Ask the Holy Spirit for Revelation**

*"Holy Spirit, I ask You to reveal any generational curses affecting my*

*life. Show me patterns of iniquity that need to be broken. Expose hidden agreements that have passed through my family line. Give me the wisdom and authority to break them in Jesus' name!"*

**Step 2:** Repent for Generational Sin and Iniquity

Generational curses remain in place because of unrepented sin in the family bloodline. Even if you did not commit the sin yourself, you can stand in the gap and repent on behalf of your ancestors—just as Daniel did for Israel (Daniel 9:4-19).

Biblical Example – Daniel's Prayer of Repentance (Daniel 9:4-6)

*"O Lord, the great and awesome God, who keeps covenant and steadfast love with those who love Him and keep His commandments, we have sinned and done wrong and acted wickedly and rebelled, turning aside from Your commandments and rules." ESV*

Daniel understood that repenting for the sins of past generations was necessary to restore favor.

Prayer of Repentance for Generational Sins:

*"Father, I come before You in the name of Jesus, and I repent for the sins of my ancestors. I renounce every act of idolatry, witchcraft, sexual sin, rebellion, and dishonor that has been in my family line. I ask for Your forgiveness and for the cleansing blood of Jesus to wash over my bloodline. Let every iniquity be broken, and let the power of every generational curse be destroyed! In Jesus' name, Amen."*

**Step 3:** Renounce the Curse and Break Its Power

Once repentance has taken place, the generational curse must be verbally renounced and broken.

### Declare Freedom Over Your Family Line

*"In the name of Jesus, I renounce every generational curse that has been operating in my bloodline. I break every cycle of poverty, sickness, addiction, and destruction. I declare that my family is no longer bound by the sins of the past! I reject and cancel every demonic assignment against my lineage, and I proclaim that we are covered by the blood of Jesus. From this day forward, my family walks in freedom and blessing! Amen!"*

**Step 4:** Destroy Any Remaining Ties to the Curse

Some generational curses are connected to physical objects, covenants, or practices that must be renounced and removed.

What to Remove:

- Occult items – Books, charms, talismans, Ouija boards, tarot cards.
- Objects tied to false religions – Statues, idols, or items used in unholy rituals.
- Items passed down through bloodlines – Some family heirlooms carry spiritual significance.
- Unholy relationships – Breaking free from toxic soul ties to people who reinforce generational sin.

Prayer to Remove Ungodly Ties:

*"Father, in Jesus' name, I renounce and destroy every object, agreement, and soul tie that has connected my family to generational curses. I reject every demonic attachment, and I command every*

*spirit linked to these items to leave now! I dedicate my household to You, and I declare that my home is filled with Your presence. Amen!"*

**Step 5:** Replace the Curse with Generational Blessing

After breaking the curse, you must replace it with God's blessing. Deuteronomy 7:9 says:

*"Know therefore that the Lord your God is God, the faithful God who keeps covenant and steadfast love with those who love Him and keep His commandments, to a thousand generations." ESV*

God desires to bless your family for generations!

Declare the Blessing of the Lord Over Your Family:

*"I declare that my family is no longer under the power of the curse but walks in the blessing of the Lord! We are blessed in our coming and going. My children and future generations will serve the Lord. Sickness, poverty, and destruction will not touch my bloodline! The favor and prosperity of the Lord are upon us, and we will leave a legacy of righteousness in Jesus' name!"*

Key Scriptures for Generational Blessing:

- Deuteronomy 28:1-14 – The blessing of obedience.
- Psalm 112:2 – "His descendants will be mighty on earth; the generation of the upright will be blessed."
- Isaiah 61:9 – "Their offspring shall be known among the nations, and their descendants in the midst of the peoples; all who see them shall acknowledge them, that they are an offspring the Lord has blessed."

**Your Family's Legacy Has Changed!**

Breaking a generational curse is not just about stopping the enemy's work—it is about starting a new legacy of faith, blessing, and abundance.

**Final Steps to Walk in Generational Blessing:**

1. Pray Over Your Family Daily – Cover your children and future generations in prayer.
2. Teach Your Family God's Ways – Establish biblical values in your home.
3. Speak Life Over Your Household – Declare blessing over your family.
4. Live in Faith and Obedience – Continue walking in righteousness.

**Final Declaration:**

*"From this day forward, my family is free from every generational curse! We walk in the divine blessing of the Lord. The chains of the past are broken, and my children and future generations will serve God. We will be known as a family of righteousness, faith, and supernatural favor! In Jesus' name, Amen!"*

# 9

# THE LIFESTYLE OF BLESSING

B reaking curses is only the beginning—God's ultimate desire is for His people to walk in a lifestyle of blessing. Many people experience temporary breakthroughs but fail to maintain lasting victory because they do not cultivate a life aligned with God's Word, truth, and relationships. Deuteronomy 28:1-2 makes it clear:

*"If you faithfully obey the voice of the Lord your God, being careful to do all His commandments that I command you today, the Lord your God will set you high above all the nations of the earth. And all these blessings shall come upon you and overtake you, if you obey the voice of the Lord your God." ESV*

This chapter will explore three key principles that ensure you walk in continual blessing:

1. Obedience to God's Word – Living under the promises of Deuteronomy 28.
2. Aligning Your Words with God's Truth – Speaking life instead of curses.

3.  Breaking Free from Toxic Influences – Surrounding yourself with faith-filled relationships.

By applying these principles, you will not only remain free from curses but also walk in supernatural favor, protection, and increase.

1. Obedience to God's Word – Living Under the Blessing of Deuteronomy 28

God's blessings are not random—they are the direct result of obedience. Throughout Scripture, God connects obedience to divine favor and protection. Deuteronomy 28:1-14 – The Blessing of Obedience

God outlines the incredible benefits of obeying His Word:

- Prosperity and success – "Blessed shall be the fruit of your womb and the fruit of your ground and the fruit of your cattle" (v. 4).
- Divine protection – "The Lord will cause your enemies who rise against you to be defeated before you" (v. 7).
- Supernatural provision – "The Lord will command the blessing on you in your barns and in all that you undertake" (v. 8).
- Influence and leadership – "The Lord will make you the head and not the tail" (v. 13).

**Why Obedience Leads to Blessing**

1.  Obedience Aligns You with God's Favor – When we walk in God's ways, we step into the flow of His blessing.

2. Obedience Closes Doors to the Enemy – Rebellion and sin give the enemy access, but obedience keeps doors shut.

3. Obedience Invites Divine Protection – When we follow God's commands, He rebukes the devourer on our behalf (Malachi 3:11).

How to Walk in Obedience Daily:

- Read and meditate on God's Word (Joshua 1:8).
- Follow the promptings of the Holy Spirit (John 16:13).
- Reject compromise and live righteously (1 Peter 1:15-16).
- Honor God with your finances, relationships, and lifestyle (Proverbs 3:9-10).

Prayer for a Life of Obedience:

*"Father, I commit to walking in obedience to Your Word. Help me to hear Your voice clearly and follow Your ways. I desire to live under the full blessing of Deuteronomy 28, and I reject every temptation to compromise. Strengthen me to walk in righteousness, holiness, and faithfulness, in Jesus' name. Amen."*

2. Aligning Your Words with God's Truth – Speaking Life Instead of Curses

Your words shape your reality. Many believers unknowingly reinforce curses by speaking negativity, doubt, or fear over themselves. The Bible teaches that words are spiritual containers that either release blessing or bondage. Proverbs 18:21 – The Power of the Tongue

*"Death and life are in the power of the tongue, and those who love it will eat its fruits." ESV*

What You Speak, You Create:

- If you constantly say, "I never have enough", you reinforce lack.
- If you declare, "I always get sick", you open the door to affliction.
- If you say, "I am not good enough", you partner with rejection and insecurity.

**Replacing Curses with Blessings**

Instead of speaking negatively, replace your words with God's truth:

- Instead of "I always struggle", say: "I am blessed and highly favored" (Luke 1:28).
- Instead of "I am afraid", declare: "God has not given me a spirit of fear" (2 Timothy 1:7).
- Instead of "Nothing ever works for me", speak: "I am the head and not the tail" (Deuteronomy 28:13).

**Daily Confessions for Blessing and Favor**

Speak these over yourself every morning:

1. "I am blessed in my coming and going" (Deuteronomy 28:6).
2. "God supplies all my needs" (Philippians 4:19).
3. "I have the mind of Christ" (1 Corinthians 2:16).
4. "No weapon formed against me shall prosper" (Isaiah 54:17).

Prayer to Align Your Words with Truth:

*"Lord, I renounce every negative word I have spoken over my life. I cancel every word curse in Jesus' name. I choose to align my speech with Your truth. Let my words reflect faith, victory, and blessing. Let my tongue be used to declare Your promises daily. Amen."*

**3.** Breaking Free from Toxic Influences – Walking in Faith-Filled Relationships

Many people struggle to maintain a lifestyle of blessing because they stay connected to the wrong people. 1 Corinthians 15:33 – The Influence of Relationships

*"Do not be deceived: 'Bad company ruins good morals.'" ESV*

Toxic relationships can keep you tied to old strongholds, fear, doubt, and negative cycles. To walk in blessing, you must surround yourself with people who strengthen your faith.

Three Types of People to Avoid:

1. People Who Speak Negativity – Those who constantly complain, gossip, or doubt.
2. People Who Encourage Sin – Friends who lead you into compromise or rebellion.
3. People Who Do Not Align with Your Calling – Those who discourage your faith and purpose.

Three Types of People to Pursue:

1. Faith-Builders – People who encourage you in Christ.
2. Mentors – Those who can guide and disciple you.

3. Godly Friends – Relationships that sharpen and strengthen you.

Prayer for Healthy Relationships:

*"Father, I ask You to remove every toxic relationship that is hindering my walk with You. Connect me with people who will strengthen my faith and encourage my spiritual growth. Help me to walk in wisdom in every relationship. In Jesus' name, Amen."*

## Walking in Continuous Blessing

A lifestyle of blessing requires:

- Obedience to God's Word – Living according to His commands.
- Aligning Your Words with Truth – Speaking life instead of curses.
- Surrounding Yourself with Godly People – Breaking free from toxic influences.

If you commit to these principles, blessing will not just visit you—it will follow you!

## Final Declaration:

*"I choose to live a life of obedience, faith, and blessing! I reject every negative word and align myself with God's promises. I walk in divine favor, provision, and protection. My relationships are healthy, my words are life-giving, and my life reflects the goodness of God! In Jesus' name, Amen!"*

## Next Steps:

- Memorize Deuteronomy 28:1-14 – The blessings of obedience.
- Commit to daily faith confessions – Speak life over yourself.
- Assess your relationships – Remove toxic influences and pursue godly connections.

# 10

## MAINTAINING YOUR FREEDOM

Breaking curses and stepping into a lifestyle of blessing is a powerful victory, but maintaining that freedom requires intentionality. The enemy will attempt to reclaim lost ground, and if you are not vigilant, old patterns can try to resurface. However, through prayer, fasting, and a lifestyle of worship, you can ensure that no curse, no bondage, and no attack of the enemy can take root again.

*"For freedom Christ has set us free; stand firm therefore, and do not submit again to a yoke of slavery." Galatians 5:1 ESV*

Freedom is not just about breaking chains—it is about walking in lasting victory. This chapter will cover three key principles for maintaining your deliverance:

1. Staying Vigilant Against Spiritual Attacks
2. Continual Renewal Through Prayer and Fasting
3. The Power of Worship and Thanksgiving
4. If you apply these principles, you will remain

unshaken, protected, and walking in supernatural favor.

**I.** Staying Vigilant Against Spiritual Attacks

The moment you step into freedom, the enemy will look for ways to pull you back. Jesus warned about this in Matthew 12:43-45:

> *"When the unclean spirit has gone out of a person, it passes through waterless places seeking rest, but finds none. Then it says, 'I will return to my house from which I came.' And when it comes, it finds the house empty, swept, and put in order. Then it goes and brings with it seven other spirits more evil than itself, and they enter and dwell there. And the last state of that person is worse than the first." ESV*

How Does the Enemy Try to Re-Enter?

- Through Old Habits and Sin – Temptation to return to past behaviors.
- Through Negative Thoughts – Doubt, fear, and condemnation.
- Through Unforgiveness – Allowing bitterness to take root.
- Through Emotional Weakness – Attacks when you are tired or discouraged.

How to Guard Your Freedom:

1. Stay in the Word of God Daily – Fill yourself with truth so there is no room for lies (Psalm 119:11).
2. Reject Thoughts of Condemnation – Do not allow guilt or shame to open a door (Romans 8:1).

3. Keep Your Mind Focused on Christ – Fix your eyes on Jesus and stay spiritually alert (Colossians 3:2).

Prayer for Spiritual Protection:

*"Father, I thank You for setting me free. I take authority over every attack of the enemy, and I declare that no weapon formed against me shall prosper. I put on the full armor of God, and I stand firm in my victory. My mind is renewed, my spirit is strong, and my heart is filled with faith. I will not return to bondage, in Jesus' name! Amen."*

**2.** Continual Renewal Through Prayer and Fasting

**Prayer: Your Spiritual Weapon**

Prayer is not just communication with God—it is a weapon of spiritual warfare. Without prayer, you leave yourself open to attack and deception.

*"Praying at all times in the Spirit, with all prayer and supplication."*
Ephesians 6:18 ESV

How to Maintain a Strong Prayer Life:

- Pray daily and consistently – Do not wait for problems to pray (1 Thessalonians 5:17).
- Pray in the Spirit – Speaking in tongues strengthens your inner man (Jude 1:20).
- Use the Word in Prayer – Declare Scripture over your life (Isaiah 55:11).

**Fasting: Unlocking Supernatural Strength**

Fasting disconnects you from worldly distractions and aligns you with the power of God.

*"Is not this the fast that I choose: to loose the bonds of wickedness, to undo the straps of the yoke, to let the oppressed go free, and to break every yoke?" Isaiah 58:6 ESV*

When to Fast:

- When facing spiritual battles.
- When seeking greater intimacy with God.
- When needing clarity or breakthrough.

Prayer to Strengthen Your Prayer and Fasting Life:

*"Lord, give me a hunger for Your presence. Teach me to pray with power and authority. Help me to fast and seek You with all my heart. Let my spirit be strong and my faith unshakable. In Jesus' name, Amen."*

**3.** The Power of Worship and Thanksgiving

Worship is more than just singing—it is a weapon against darkness. The enemy cannot remain where there is true, Spirit-filled worship.

*"Yet You are holy, enthroned on the praises of Israel." Psalm 22:3 ESV*

When you fill your home, your mind, and your heart with worship, you are creating an atmosphere where the presence of God dwells.

**The Power of Thanksgiving**

Thanksgiving keeps your heart focused on the goodness of God. Many people lose their deliverance because they start complaining, doubting, or forgetting what God has done.

"Rejoice always, pray without ceasing, give thanks in all circumstances; for this is the will of God in Christ Jesus for you." 1 Thessalonians 5:16-18 ESV

How to Maintain a Lifestyle of Worship and Thanksgiving:

- Start every day with gratitude.
- Play worship music in your home.
- Sing praises even in difficult moments.

Declaration of Worship and Thanksgiving:

*"I will bless the Lord at all times; His praise will continually be in my mouth! I choose to worship and give thanks, no matter what I face. I declare that my home and my life are filled with the presence of God. Amen!"*

Lasting Freedom is Yours!

If you commit to:

- Staying vigilant against spiritual attacks
- Living a lifestyle of prayer and fasting
- Filling your life with worship and thanksgiving

...you will remain in complete and total freedom.

**Final Declarations:**

- I will not return to bondage!
- I will walk in victory daily!
- I will live a life of prayer and faith!
- I will worship God and remain thankful in all things!

## Next Steps: Preparing for Generational Blessing

Now that you are free and walking in blessing, it's time to pass it on! In the next chapter, we will explore how to bless others, release favor, and establish a legacy of faith.

Your life is no longer cursed—you are now a carrier of blessing! Keep walking in victory!

# 11

---

## BLESSING OTHERS AND RELEASING FAVOR

Walking in the blessing of God is not just about personal freedom—it is about becoming a source of blessing to others. When God blesses someone, His intent is that the blessing will flow through them to impact their family, community, and even the nations.

*"I will make you into a great nation, and I will bless you; I will make your name great, and you will be a blessing." Genesis 12:2 NIV*

God's kingdom operates on the principle of multiplication. Just as curses can pass down generationally, blessings can also be transferred and released. This chapter will equip you to:

1. Understand the authority you have to bless.
2. Speak life over your family, business, and ministry.
3. Use prophetic declarations to shape your future.

When you grasp this, you will no longer only receive blessing—you will release it wherever you go!

## 1. The Authority of a Believer to Bless

Many people do not realize that they have the authority to bless others. In the Old Testament, blessings were spoken by fathers, prophets, and priests, but in Christ, every believer carries the power to bless.

### 1 Peter 2:9 – You Are a Royal Priesthood

*"But you are a chosen race, a royal priesthood, a holy nation, a people for his own possession, that you may proclaim the excellencies of Him who called you out of darkness into His marvelous light." ESV*

As a king and priest in Christ, you have the power to:

- Speak blessings over your family, business, and future.
- Declare prosperity, healing, and protection.
- Release favor and increase over others.

Biblical Example: The Power of Spoken Blessing

- Isaac blessed Jacob (Genesis 27:27-29).
- Aaron was commanded to bless Israel (Numbers 6:24-26).
- Jesus blessed children and His disciples (Mark 10:16, Luke 24:50).

If blessings could shape destinies in the Bible, they can do the same today. You are called to release life-giving words over yourself and those around you.

Declaration of Authority:

*"In Jesus' name, I take my rightful place as a child of God. I have the power to bless, and I will use my words to release life, favor, and increase. My life is a source of blessing to my family, my community, and my generation!"*

**2.** Speaking Life Over Your Family, Business, and Ministry

Your words are a prophetic seed. When you speak, you are either sowing blessings or curses into your future.

Proverbs 18:21 – The Power of Words

*"Death and life are in the power of the tongue, and those who love it will eat its fruit." ESV*

How to Speak Blessing Over Key Areas of Your Life:

1. Blessing Your Family

Declare:

*"My family is covered under the blood of Jesus. My household walks in divine favor, health, and prosperity. My children are strong in the Lord and will fulfill their purpose in Christ. No weapon formed against my family shall prosper!"*

2. Blessing Your Finances and Business

Declare:

*"The Lord is my provider. I have more than enough to meet my needs and to be a blessing to others. My business prospers, and every financial curse is broken. Wealth and resources flow freely into my hands because I am a faithful steward."*

## 3. Blessing Your Ministry and Calling

Declare:

*"I am anointed and appointed for such a time as this. I will walk in my purpose and fulfill my destiny. Doors of opportunity open before me, and I am surrounded by divine connections. My ministry impacts lives, and I will leave a legacy for generations to come!"*

Speaking these blessings daily creates an atmosphere of faith that invites God's presence into every area of your life.

## 3. Using Prophetic Declarations to Shape Your Future

What Are Prophetic Declarations?

Prophetic declarations are Spirit-led words spoken in faith that align with God's promises. They are based on biblical truths and activate God's power over your life. Isaiah 55:11 says:

*"So shall my word be that goes out from my mouth; it shall not return to me empty, but it shall accomplish that which I purpose, and shall succeed in the thing for which I sent it." ESV*

God's Word is a creative force—when spoken in faith, it brings transformation.

How to Make Prophetic Declarations:

1. Base them on Scripture – Every declaration should align with God's promises.
2. Speak them with boldness – Say them aloud and believe them.

3. Declare them consistently – Speak blessings over your life daily.

Examples of Prophetic Declarations:

- "I am blessed and highly favored!" (Luke 1:28)
- "I am the head and not the tail, above and not beneath!" (Deuteronomy 28:13)
- "I walk in divine health and healing!" (Isaiah 53:5)
- "Every plan of the enemy against me is destroyed!" (Isaiah 54:17)
- "I am fruitful, prosperous, and walking in supernatural increase!" (Psalm 1:3)

As you declare these promises, your faith is activated, and heaven responds!

## You Are a Carrier of Blessing

Breaking curses was just the beginning—now you are a vessel of God's favor!

## Final Commitments to Live a Life of Blessing:

- I will use my words to release life and favor.
- I will bless my family, business, and ministry daily.
- I will declare God's promises over my future.
- I will be a source of blessing to others.

## Final Declaration:

*"I am no longer under a curse—I am under the blessing of God! My words carry power, and I will speak life, favor, and increase. I bless*

*my family, my finances, and my future. I am a light in my generation, and I will impact lives for the Kingdom of God. In Jesus' name, Amen!"*

## Next Steps: Walking in Generational Blessing

- Pray daily for God's favor over your life.
- Bless your family, business, and ministry every morning.
- Speak prophetic declarations over your future.
- Teach others how to walk in blessing and release favor.

## Closing Challenge:

Now that you are walking in freedom and blessing, ask yourself:

- Who in my life can I bless today?
- How can I use my testimony to encourage others?
- What legacy of faith will I leave for future generations?

Your journey is just beginning—go and be a blessing!

# CONCLUSION
## CHOOSE LIFE AND BLESSING

You have come to the end of this book, but your journey into lasting freedom and blessing is just beginning. God has set before you two paths—one of life and blessing, the other of death and curse. The choice is yours.

*"I call heaven and earth to witness against you today, that I have set before you life and death, blessing and curse. Therefore choose life, that you and your offspring may live." Deuteronomy 30:19 ESV*

You are no longer bound by generational curses, spoken word curses, or past failures. Jesus has redeemed you from the curse and made you a carrier of His blessing (Galatians 3:13-14). Now, you must consciously walk in that blessing every day.

This conclusion will serve as a final reminder of how to:

- Stand on God's promises
- Make the daily choice to walk in blessing
- Declare lasting breakthrough over your life

Making the Conscious Choice to Walk in Blessing

## 1. Walk in Obedience

Blessing is not random—it is connected to obedience.

*"And if you faithfully obey the voice of the Lord your God, being careful to do all His commandments... all these blessings shall come upon you and overtake you." Deuteronomy 28:1-2 ESV*

Your daily choice:

- Obey God's commands.
- Live a life of integrity and holiness.
- Keep your heart free from sin, bitterness, and rebellion.

## 2. Keep Your Mind and Words Aligned with God's Truth

The enemy will always try to pull you back into old thinking. You must choose to renew your mind daily.

- Speak blessings, not curses.
- Reject fear, doubt, and negativity.
- Declare God's promises boldly.

*"Do not be conformed to this world, but be transformed by the renewal of your mind, that by testing you may discern what is the will of God, what is good and acceptable and perfect." Romans 12:2 ESV*

## 3. Stay in Prayer and Worship

Freedom is maintained through intimacy with God.

- Pray daily.
- Fast regularly.
- Surround yourself with worship.

*"Rejoice always, pray without ceasing, give thanks in all circumstances; for this is the will of God in Christ Jesus for you." 1 Thessalonians 5:16-18 ESV*

## 4. Surround Yourself with Faith-Filled People

Your environment matters. Stay connected to people of faith who encourage, challenge, and strengthen you.

- Find a strong church community.
- Be mentored and mentor others.
- Reject relationships that pull you back into sin.

*"Whoever walks with the wise becomes wise, but the companion of fools will suffer harm." Proverbs 13:20 ESV*

## 5. Pass the Blessing to Future Generations

You are not just walking in blessing for yourself—you are establishing a new legacy.

- Pray over your children and grandchildren.
- Teach biblical values in your home.
- Declare blessings over your household.

*"His descendants will be mighty on earth; the generation of the upright will be blessed." Psalm 112:2 ESV*

**Prayers and Declarations for Lasting Breakthrough**

Now, let's seal everything with prayer and declaration.

**Final Prayer of Blessing:**

*"Father, I thank You for delivering me from every curse and bringing me into a life of blessing. I choose to walk in obedience, faith, and victory. I reject every lie of the enemy and align my mind with Your Word. My family, my future, and my purpose are covered under the blood of Jesus. I will leave a legacy of righteousness, favor, and abundance. From this day forward, I will walk in divine blessing and never return to bondage. In Jesus' name, Amen!"*

**Final Declarations of Blessing:**

Declare these over yourself every day:

- I am blessed and highly favored! (Luke 1:28)
- I am the head and not the tail, above and not beneath! (Deuteronomy 28:13)
- I walk in divine health, healing, and prosperity! (Isaiah 53:5)
- Every plan of the enemy against me is destroyed! (Isaiah 54:17)
- My family is covered under the blood of Jesus! (Exodus 12:13)
- I am a child of God, and I walk in supernatural victory! (Romans 8:37)

**Final Challenge: Choose Blessing Every Day**

You are now equipped to live in blessing and to release blessing wherever you go. Every day, you will face a choice:

- To walk in faith or live in fear

- To speak life or speak defeat
- To align with God's truth or believe the enemy's lies

**CHOOSE LIFE. CHOOSE BLESSING. CHOOSE VICTORY.**

Now go forth and walk in everything God has prepared for you!

**Next Steps: Walking in Generational Blessing**

- Memorize Deuteronomy 28:1-14 – The blessings of obedience.
- Speak blessings over your life daily – Declare God's promises.
- Stay connected to faith-filled believers – Find a strong church community.
- Teach others what you've learned – Help break curses in others' lives.

Your Journey Continues...

You are no longer cursed—you are a carrier of blessing. Your testimony will impact generations, and your legacy will be one of faith, favor, and victory. Walk boldly in your calling, and let your life be a beacon of God's goodness!

The best is yet to come. Keep walking in blessing!

# ABOUT THE AUTHOR

Tom Cornell is the Senior Leader of SOZO Church in Washington state, founder of Walk in the Light International and SOZO Network. Tom is married to his beautiful wife Katy and lives in the Puget Sound area with her and their three kids. He has been in ministry pastoring and teaching the body of Christ since 2008.

He has a passion to see the body of Christ moving from people with an orphan mindset to that of sonship; equipping the body to do the work of Jesus resulting in seeing the Kingdom of God manifested here on earth.

www.ingramcontent.com/pod-product-compliance
Lightning Source LLC
LaVergne TN
LVHW052036080426
835513LV00018B/2356

* 9 7 8 1 9 6 9 8 8 2 0 9 8 *